African Rhinos

By Alison Tibbitts and
Alan Roocroft

PUBLISHED BY
Capstone Press
Mankato, Minnesota USA

CIP
LIBRARY OF CONGRESS CATALOGING IN PUBLICATION DATA

Tibbitts, Alison.
    African rhinos / by Alison Tibbitts and Alan Roocroft.
        p. cm. -- (Animals, animals, animals)
    Summary: Describes the physical characteristics, behavior, and life cycle of the two African species of rhinoceros.

    ISBN 1-56065-101-6
    1. Black rhinoceros--Juvenile literature. 2. White rhinoceros--Juvenile literature. 3. Rhinoceroses--Africa--Juvenile literature.
[1. Black rhinoceros. 2. White rhinoceros. 3. Rhinoceroses--Africa.]
I. Roocroft, Alan. II. Title. III. Series: Tibbitts, Alison. Animals, animals, animals.
    QL737.U63T53   1992
    599.72'8--dc20
                              92-11440
                              CIP
                              AC

Consultant:
Rick Barongi, Director, Children's Zoo
Zoological Society of San Diego

Photo Credits:
Alison Tibbitts and Alan Roocroft

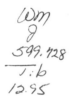

Capstone Press
P.O. Box 669, Mankato, MN, U.S.A. 56002-0669

Sun beats down on the African plain. Large rocks lie partly submerged in a shallow pond. Birds pick ticks and insects off the boulders. In time, one rock stands up and walks away. Another follows. The rhinoceroses are leaving their **wallow**.

Rhinos trace back over a million years. They once ranged through Europe, Asia, North America, and Africa. Woolly rhinos wore long blankets of hair. Drawings of rhinos decorated walls in ancient caves. The animals appeared in Roman circuses. Their name comes from two Greek words, rhino and ceros, meaning "nose horn."

Africa is home to black and white rhinos. They are alike in many but not all ways. Both have wrinkled gray skin. Hair **fringes** their ears and tails. Toes end in three separate hooves. Their two horns are used as tools and weapons. A group of rhinos is called a "crash."

A big difference between African rhinos is the shape of their mouths. This affects what they eat and where they live. White rhinos have wide, square lips for **grazing**. Black rhinos have a hooked upper lip, called a **prehensile** lip, for **browsing**.

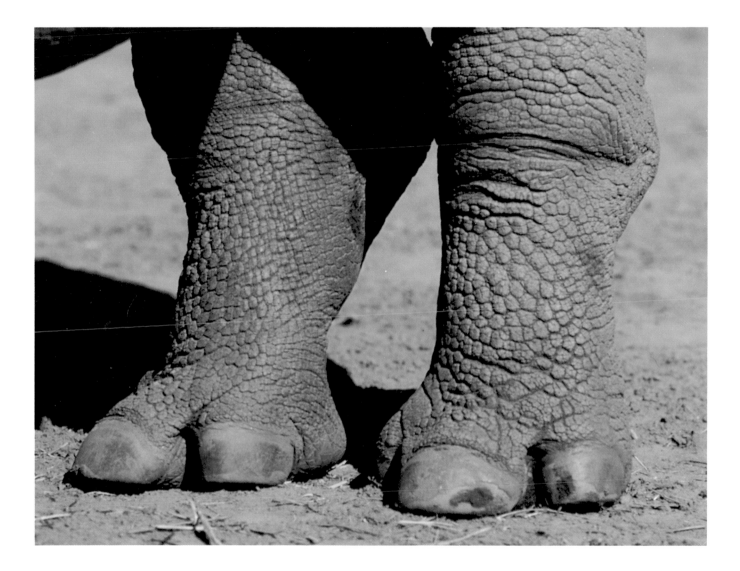

White rhinos eat short grass on the open plains. They stand the same way whether they are grazing or not. Their heads bend low as they walk. The front horn develops a flat surface from being rubbed against the ground.

Black rhinos live along the edges of small woodlands. They eat bushes and small trees. They use their horns to pull down and break branches. The prehensile lip wraps around leaves, twigs, and fruit. It pulls new plants from the ground. This opens more grasslands for grazing animals.

Rhinos lift their feet gracefully when they **trot**. They move like their closest relative, the horse. Rhinos' sense of smell is good. Their vision is poor. A black rhino may charge if it is surprised or threatened. It might be serious or it could be bluffing. White rhinos are more calm than black rhinos.

White rhinos behave according to their sex and place in the **social order**. They pick a fight with another rhino to test their strength. This is not intended to hurt anyone. The **aggressor** raises his tail in the air. His legs stiffen. He snorts, paws the ground, and charges. The two butt heads and wrestle with their horns. In time, one loses interest and wanders away.

Territory is closely guarded by white rhinos. Each **dominant** male rules his feeding area. Other adult males may not graze unless they give in to him. They must make the proper sounds and gestures of **submission**. Black rhinos are not **territorial** about feeding areas.

Females need larger feeding areas to support their **calves**. The size depends on how many animals live there and how much food they need. **Cows** with babies usually get along well.

Water holes are important. White rhinos go no more than six miles away from water. They drink every couple of days. Black rhinos stay within three miles of permanent water. They need to drink every day.

Wallowing goes on daily at the water holes. Rhinos lie in the mud for hours. This cools their skin and keeps it safe from insect bites. White rhinos graze around their water holes. The short grass gives less cover to predators waiting for calves. A group of six or eight male black rhinos wallow together. Although these males are **solitary**, they know and tolerate each other well. Outsiders must be accepted before they may join the group in the wallow.

Many animals travel by old rhino paths and tunnels in the vegetation. This saves the trouble of making new ones. Black rhinos crash noisily through the bush. They make no secret of their presence. They avoid only elephants and humans. Adult rhinos have no **predators** except man.

White rhinos make many sounds. They cough, whine, squeal, fierce bellow, low growl, and chirp. The meaning depends on the situation. A rhino fight is a rare and bellowing event. Courting males' **hic-throbbings** can be heard through the ground over a long distance. Black rhinos have only a few squeals to communicate their purpose.

Rhinos leave scent messages for each other. They spray urine to mark territory. They add to dung heaps for the same reason. These heaps tell how many animals have used the trails and when. Passing rhinos have a social duty to add to the pile. Only the dominate male kicks the heaps in his territory.

Breeding takes place every three or four years. A cow has her first calf at about seven. She could have six or eight during her thirty- to forty-year lifetime. Courtship is a long process. A male responds to a female. He bellows and chases her. She resists violently. He is threatened by her and her possessive young calf. It is a noisy and tiring time.

Cows give birth to a single calf after sixteen months. The baby walks within an hour. Cow and calf stay in deep cover during the first two weeks. A newborn follows his mother closely. An older calf walks just ahead of her.

A white rhino cow chases her calf away when she has another one. He joins a childless "auntie" or another calf of his own age. Several may form a kind of youth club. These calves might stay together for several years. Dominant males allow them to feed in his territory because they do not threaten his control.

Horns are hard, **fibrous keratin** mixed with matted hair. A horn's size depends on where the rhino lived when it was grown. Large horns are seldom seen any more. Smaller ones come from dry climates. Females have longer, thinner horns. A calf has a flat plate on his nose where horns will develop. Some rangers protect rhinos from **poachers** by sawing off their horns. These grow back in about a year.

People in Africa and Asia have used rhinoceros horns for centuries. They grind them into powder for religious and medicinal purposes. Poachers have killed thousands of rhinos. They sold the horns to be made into dagger handles.

What is the future? Both rhinos and habitats need protection. Some countries are working on these problems. People can help by never buying rhino products.

GLOSSARY / INDEX

Aggressor: the animal who picks a fight or attacks first (page 10)

Browsing: eating tender parts of shrubs and trees (page 6)

Calves: male and female babies (page 13)

Cows: adult females more than seven years old (page 13)

Dominant: largest, strongest, most important animal in the group (page 13)

Fibrous keratin: tough strings of protein that are the basic building blocks for hair, horns, hoofs, and skin (page 22)

Fringes: decorating or trimming around the edges (page 6)

Grazing: eating grass close to the ground (page 6)

Hic-throbbing: a hiccup sound made by rhinos (page 17)

Poachers: people who break the law to kill animals and steal parts of the bodies to sell (page 22)

Predators: animals who hunt and kill other animals for food (page 17)

Prehensile: adapted for grasping or taking hold (page 6)

Social order: animals know their place in the group's organization (page 10)

Solitary: living or traveling alone, without others (page 14)

Submission: giving in to the stronger or dominant animal (page 13)

Territorial: controlling a certain area of land (page 13)

Trot: moving the legs at a speed between a walk and a run (page 10)

Wallow: a place where animals lie or roll around in the mud (page 5)